Santa's
Favorite Cookies

Sweet Treats for the Christmas Season

Brownies & Bars

Mystical Layered Bars

⅓ cup margarine or butter
1 cup graham cracker crumbs
½ cup old-fashioned or quick oats
1 can (14 ounces) sweetened condensed milk
1 cup flaked coconut
¾ cup semisweet chocolate chips
¾ cup raisins
1 cup coarsely chopped pecans

Preheat oven to 350°F. Melt margarine in 13×9-inch baking pan. Remove from oven.

Sprinkle graham cracker crumbs and oats evenly over margarine; press down with fork. Drizzle condensed milk over oats. Layer coconut, chocolate chips, raisins and pecans over milk.

continued on page 4

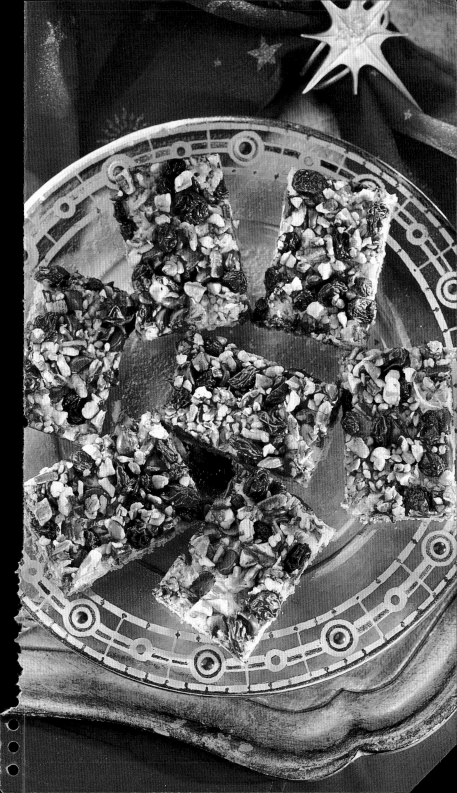

Mystical Layered Bars, continued

Bake 25 to 30 minutes or until lightly browned. Cool in pan on wire rack 5 minutes; cut into 2×1½-inch bars. Cool completely in pan on wire rack.

Store tightly covered at room temperature or freeze up to 3 months. *Makes 3 dozen bars*

Praline Brownies

Brownies

- **1 package DUNCAN HINES® Chocolate Lovers Milk Chocolate Chunk Brownie Mix**
- **2 eggs**
- **⅓ cup water**
- **⅓ cup canola oil plus additional for greasing**
- **¾ cup chopped pecans**

Topping

- **¾ cup firmly packed brown sugar**
- **¾ cup chopped pecans**
- **¼ cup butter or margarine, melted**
- **2 tablespoons milk**
- **½ teaspoon vanilla extract**

1. Preheat oven to 350°F. Grease 9-inch square pan.

2. For brownies, combine brownie mix, eggs, water, oil and ¾ cup pecans in large bowl. Stir with spoon until well blended, about 50 strokes. Spread in prepared pan. Bake at 350°F for 35 to 40 minutes. Remove from oven.

3. For topping, combine brown sugar, ¾ cup pecans, melted butter, milk and vanilla extract in medium bowl. Stir with spoon until well blended. Spread over hot brownies. Return to oven. Bake for 15 minutes longer or until topping is set. Cool completely in pan on wire rack. Cut into bars.
Makes about 16 brownies

Helpful Hint

Cut brownies and bar cookies into triangles or diamonds for a festive new look. To make serving easy, remove a corner piece first, then remove the rest.

Praline Brownies

Luscious Lemon Bars

2 lemons
2 cups all-purpose flour
1 cup butter
½ cup powdered sugar
¼ teaspoon salt
1 cup granulated sugar
3 large eggs
⅓ cup fresh lemon juice
  Sifted powdered sugar

1. Finely grate colored portion of lemon peel. Measure 4 teaspoons lemon peel; set aside.

2. Preheat oven to 350°F. Grease 13×9-inch baking pan; set aside. Place 1 teaspoon lemon peel, flour, butter, powdered sugar and salt in food processor. Process until mixture forms coarse crumbs.

3. Press mixture evenly into prepared 13×9-inch baking pan. Bake 18 to 20 minutes or until golden brown.

4. Beat remaining 3 teaspoons lemon peel, granulated sugar, eggs and lemon juice in medium bowl with electric mixer at medium speed until well blended.

5. Pour mixture evenly over warm crust. Return to oven; bake 18 to 20 minutes or until center is set and edges are golden brown. Remove pan to wire rack; cool completely.

6. Dust with sifted powdered sugar; cut into 2×1½-inch bars.

7. Store tightly covered at room temperature. Do not freeze.

Makes 3 dozen bars

Almond Toffee Bars

¾ cup butter or margarine, softened
¾ cup packed brown sugar
1½ cups all-purpose flour
½ teaspoon almond extract
½ teaspoon vanilla extract
¼ teaspoon salt
1 package (6 ounces) semi-sweet real chocolate pieces
¾ cup BLUE DIAMOND® Chopped Natural Almonds, toasted

Preheat oven to 350°F. Cream butter and sugar; blend in flour. Add extracts and salt, mixing well. Spread in bottom of ungreased 13×9×2-inch baking pan. Bake in 350°F oven for 15 to 20 minutes or until deep golden brown. Remove from oven and sprinkle with chocolate pieces. When chocolate has melted, spread evenly; sprinkle with almonds. Cut into bars; cool.

Makes about 40 bars

Luscious Lemon Bars

Raspberry & White Chip Nut Bars

1⅔ cups (10-ounce package) **HERSHEY'S Premier White Chips, divided**
¾ cup (1½ sticks) butter or margarine
2¼ cups all-purpose flour
¾ cup sugar
3 eggs
¾ teaspoon baking powder
1⅔ cups (10-ounce package) **HERSHEY'S Raspberry Chips, divided**
½ cup chopped pecans
Double Drizzle (recipe follows)

1. Heat oven to 350°F. Grease 13×9×2-inch baking pan.

2. Reserve 2 tablespoons white chips for drizzle. In medium microwave-safe bowl, place remaining white chips and butter. Microwave at HIGH (100%) 1½ minutes; stir. If necessary, microwave at HIGH an additional 15 seconds at a time, stirring after each heating, just until chips are melted when stirred. In large bowl, combine flour, sugar, eggs and baking powder. Add white chip mixture; beat well. Reserve 2 tablespoons raspberry chips for drizzle. Chop remaining raspberry chips in food processor (use pulsing motion); stir into batter with pecans. Spread batter into prepared pan.

3. Bake 25 minutes or until edges pull away from sides of pan and top surface is golden. Cool completely in pan on wire rack. Prepare Double Drizzle; using one flavor at a time, drizzle over top of bars. Cut into bars.
Makes about 24 bars

Double Drizzle: In small microwave-safe bowl, place 2 tablespoons HERSHEY'S Premier White Chips and ½ teaspoon shortening (do not use butter, margarine or oil). Microwave at HIGH (100%) 1 minute; stir. If necessary, microwave at HIGH an additional 15 seconds at a time, stirring after each heating, just until chips are melted when stirred. Repeat procedure with raspberry chips.

Peanut Butter and Chocolate Bars: Omit HERSHEY'S Premier White Chips; replace with REESE'S® Peanut Butter Chips. Omit HERSHEY'S Raspberry Chips; replace with HERSHEY'S Semi-Sweet Chocolate Chips. Omit chopped pecans; replace with ½ cup chopped peanuts.

Cocoa Brownies

1¼ cups all-purpose flour
1 cup packed light brown
    sugar
¾ cup sugar
½ cup egg substitute
½ cup margarine or butter,
    melted
¼ cup unsweetened cocoa
1½ teaspoons vanilla extract
⅓ cup PLANTERS® Pecans,
    chopped
Powdered sugar

1. Mix flour, sugars, egg substitute, melted margarine or butter and cocoa in large bowl until well blended. Stir in vanilla and pecans.

2. Spread in well greased 13×9×2-inch baking pan. Bake in preheated 350°F oven for 25 minutes or until done. Cool in pan on wire rack. Dust with powdered sugar; cut into bars.

Makes 3 dozen

Preparation Time: 20 minutes
Cook Time: 25 minutes
Total Time: 45 minutes

Marshmallow Krispie Bars

1 package DUNCAN HINES®
    Chocolate Lovers Fudge
    Brownie Mix, Family Size
1 package (10½ ounces)
    miniature marshmallows
1½ cups semi-sweet chocolate
    chips
1 cup creamy peanut butter
1 tablespoon butter or
    margarine
1½ cups crisp rice cereal

1. Preheat oven to 350°F. Grease bottom of 13×9-inch pan.

2. Prepare and bake brownies following package directions for basic recipe. Remove from oven. Sprinkle marshmallows on hot brownies. Return to oven. Bake for 3 minutes longer.

3. Place chocolate chips, peanut butter and butter in medium saucepan. Cook over low heat, stirring constantly, until chips are melted. Add rice cereal; mix well. Spread mixture over marshmallow layer. Refrigerate until chilled. Cut into bars.

Makes about 2 dozen bars

Tip: For a special presentation, cut cookies into diamond shapes.

Caramel Fudge Brownies

1 jar (12 ounces) hot caramel ice cream topping
1¼ cups all-purpose flour, divided
¼ teaspoon baking powder
Dash salt
4 squares (1 ounce each) unsweetened chocolate, coarsely chopped
¾ cup margarine or butter
2 cups sugar
3 eggs
2 teaspoons vanilla
¾ cup semisweet chocolate chips
¾ cup chopped pecans

Preheat oven to 350°F. Lightly grease 13×9-inch baking pan.

Combine caramel topping and ¼ cup flour in small bowl; set aside.

Combine remaining 1 cup flour, baking powder and salt in small bowl; mix well.

Place unsweetened chocolate squares and margarine in medium microwavable bowl. Microwave at HIGH 2 minutes or until margarine is melted; stir until chocolate is completely melted.

Stir sugar into melted chocolate with mixing spoon. Add eggs and vanilla; stir until combined.

Add flour mixture, stirring until well blended. Spread chocolate mixture evenly into prepared pan.

Bake 25 minutes. Immediately after removing brownies from oven, spread caramel mixture over brownies. Sprinkle top evenly with chocolate chips and pecans.

Return pan to oven; bake 20 to 25 minutes or until topping is golden brown and bubbling. (Do not overbake.) Cool brownies completely in pan on wire rack. Cut into 2×1½-inch bars.

Store tightly covered at room temperature or freeze up to 3 months.

Makes 3 dozen brownies

Helpful Hint

Always use the pan size called for in the recipe. Substituting a different pan will affect the cookies' texture, often making them too dry or cakey.

Caramel Fudge Brownies

Yuletide Linzer Bars

1⅓ cups butter or margarine, softened
¾ cup sugar
1 egg
1 teaspoon grated lemon peel
2½ cups all-purpose flour
1½ cups whole almonds, ground
1 teaspoon ground cinnamon
¾ cup raspberry preserves
Powdered sugar

Preheat oven to 350°F. Grease 13×9-inch baking pan.

Beat butter and sugar in large bowl with electric mixer until creamy. Beat in egg and lemon peel until blended. Mix in flour, almonds and cinnamon until well blended.

Press 2 cups dough into bottom of prepared pan. Spread preserves over crust. Press remaining dough, a small amount at a time, evenly over preserves.

Bake 35 to 40 minutes until golden brown. Cool in pan on wire rack. Sprinkle with powdered sugar; cut into bars.

Makes 36 bars

Supreme Chocolate Saucepan Brownies

1 cup butter or margarine
2 cups sugar
½ cup HERSHEY'S Cocoa
4 eggs, beaten
⅔ cup all-purpose flour
½ teaspoon salt
¼ teaspoon baking soda
2 teaspoons vanilla extract
2 cups (12-ounce package) HERSHEY'S Semi-Sweet Chocolate Chips
½ cup macadamia nuts, coarsely chopped

Heat oven to 350°F. Grease 13×9×2-inch baking pan.

In medium saucepan over low heat melt butter. Add sugar and cocoa; stir to blend. Remove from heat. Stir in eggs. Stir together flour, salt and baking soda; stir into chocolate mixture. Stir in vanilla, chocolate chips and nuts. Spread in prepared pan.

Bake 30 to 35 minutes or until brownies begin to pull away from sides of pan and begin to crack slightly; do not underbake. Cool completely; cut into bars.

Makes about 24 brownies

Yuletide Linzer Bars

Crimson Ribbon Bars

6 tablespoons butter or margarine, softened
½ cup firmly packed brown sugar
1 teaspoon vanilla
½ cup all-purpose flour
¼ teaspoon baking soda
1½ cups rolled oats
1 cup chopped walnuts
½ cup chopped BLUE RIBBON® Calimyrna or Mission Figs
⅓ cup SMUCKER'S® Red Raspberry Preserves

Heat oven to 375°F. Combine butter, brown sugar and vanilla; beat until well blended. Add flour and baking soda; mix well. Stir in oats and walnuts. Reserve ¾ cup mixture for topping. Press remaining oat mixture in 8-inch square baking pan. Combine figs and preserves; spread mixture to within ½ inch of edges. Sprinkle with reserved oat mixture; press lightly.

Bake for 25 to 30 minutes or until golden brown. Cool in pan; cut into bars. *Makes 20 bars*

Black Russian Brownies

4 squares (1 ounce each) unsweetened chocolate
1 cup butter
¾ teaspoon ground black pepper
4 eggs, lightly beaten
1½ cups granulated sugar
1½ teaspoons vanilla
⅓ cup KAHLÚA® Liqueur
2 tablespoons vodka
1⅓ cups all-purpose flour
½ teaspoon salt
¼ teaspoon baking powder
1 cup chopped walnuts or toasted sliced almonds
Powdered sugar (optional)

Preheat oven to 350°F. Line bottom of 13×9-inch baking pan with waxed paper. Melt chocolate and butter with pepper in small saucepan over low heat, stirring until smooth. Remove from heat; cool.

Combine eggs, granulated sugar and vanilla in large bowl; beat well. Stir in cooled chocolate mixture, Kahlua and vodka. Combine flour, salt and baking powder; add to chocolate mixture and stir until blended. Add walnuts. Spread evenly in prepared pan.

Bake just until wooden toothpick inserted into center comes out clean, about 25 minutes. *Do not overbake.* Cool in pan on wire rack. Cut into bars. Sprinkle with powdered sugar.

Makes about 2½ dozen brownies

Decadent Brownies

½ cup dark corn syrup
½ cup butter or margarine
6 squares (1 ounce each) semisweet chocolate
¾ cup sugar
3 eggs
1 cup all-purpose flour
1 cup chopped walnuts
1 teaspoon vanilla
   Fudge Glaze (recipe follows)

Preheat oven to 350°F. Grease an 8-inch square pan. Combine corn syrup, butter and chocolate in large heavy saucepan. Place over low heat; stir until chocolate is melted and ingredients are blended. Remove from heat; blend in sugar. Stir in eggs, flour, chopped walnuts and vanilla. Spread batter evenly in prepared pan.

Bake 20 to 25 minutes or just until center is set. (Do not overbake.) Meanwhile, prepare Fudge Glaze. Remove brownies from oven. Immediately spread glaze evenly over hot brownies. Cool in pan on wire rack. Cut into 2-inch squares.

Makes 16 brownies

Fudge Glaze

3 squares (1 ounce each) semisweet chocolate
2 tablespoons dark corn syrup
1 tablespoon butter or margarine
1 teaspoon light cream or milk

Combine chocolate, corn syrup and butter in small heavy saucepan. Stir over low heat until chocolate is melted; mix in cream.

Triple Chocolate Brownies

3 squares (1 ounce each)
  unsweetened chocolate,
  coarsely chopped
2 squares (1 ounce each)
  semisweet chocolate,
  coarsely chopped
½ cup butter
1 cup all-purpose flour
½ teaspoon salt
¼ teaspoon baking powder
1½ cups sugar
3 large eggs
1 teaspoon vanilla
¼ cup sour cream
½ cup milk chocolate chips
  Powdered sugar (optional)

Preheat oven to 350°F. Lightly grease 13×9-inch baking pan.

Place unsweetened chocolate, semisweet chocolate and butter in medium microwavable bowl. Microwave at HIGH 2 minutes or until butter is melted; stir until chocolate is completely melted. Cool to room temperature.

Place flour, salt and baking powder in small bowl; stir to combine.

Beat sugar, eggs and vanilla in large bowl with electric mixer at medium speed until slightly thickened. Beat in chocolate mixture until well combined. Add flour mixture; beat at low speed until blended. Add sour cream; beat at low speed until combined. Stir in milk chocolate chips. Spread mixture evenly into prepared pan.

Bake 20 to 25 minutes or until toothpick inserted into center comes out almost clean. (Do not overbake.) Cool brownies completely in pan on wire rack. Cut into 2-inch squares. Place powdered sugar in fine-mesh strainer; sprinkle over brownies, if desired.

Store tightly covered at room temperature or freeze up to 3 months.

Makes 2 dozen brownies

Triple Chocolate Brownies

Cookie Jar Classics

Peanut Butter Chocolate Chippers

1 cup creamy or chunky peanut butter
1 cup firmly packed light brown sugar
1 egg
¾ cup milk chocolate chips
Granulated sugar

Preheat oven to 350°F. Mix peanut butter, sugar and egg in bowl. Stir in chips. Roll dough into 1½-inch balls. Place on ungreased cookie sheets. Dip fork in granulated sugar; press onto each ball, flattening to ½-inch thickness. Bake 12 minutes or until set. Let cookies stand on cookie sheets 2 minutes. Transfer to wire racks.

Makes about 2 dozen cookies

Note: This simple recipe is unusual because it doesn't contain any flour—but it still makes great cookies!

Mocha Crinkles

1⅓ **cups firmly packed light brown sugar**
½ **cup vegetable oil**
¼ **cup low-fat sour cream**
1 **egg**
1 **teaspoon vanilla**
1¾ **cups all-purpose flour**
¾ **cup unsweetened cocoa powder**
2 **teaspoons instant espresso or coffee granules**
1 **teaspoon baking soda**
¼ **teaspoon salt**
⅛ **teaspoon ground black pepper**
½ **cup powdered sugar**

1. Beat brown sugar and oil in medium bowl with electric mixer. Mix in sour cream, egg and vanilla. Set aside.

2. Mix flour, cocoa, espresso, baking soda, salt and pepper in another medium bowl.

3. Add flour mixture to brown sugar mixture; mix well. Refrigerate dough until firm, 3 to 4 hours.

4. Preheat oven to 350°F. Pour powdered sugar into shallow bowl. Set aside. Cut dough into 1-inch pieces; roll into balls. Roll balls in powdered sugar.

5. Bake on ungreased cookie sheets 10 to 12 minutes or until tops of cookies are firm to touch. (Do not overbake.) Cool on wire racks. *Makes 6 dozen*

Spicy Oatmeal Raisin Cookies

1 **package DUNCAN HINES® Moist Deluxe Spice Cake Mix**
4 **egg whites**
1 **cup quick-cooking oats (not instant or old-fashioned), uncooked**
½ **cup canola oil**
½ **cup raisins**

1. Preheat oven to 350°F. Grease cookie sheets.

2. Combine cake mix, egg whites, oats and oil in large mixer bowl. Beat on low speed with electric mixer until blended. Stir in raisins. Drop by rounded teaspoons onto prepared cookie sheets.

3. Bake 7 to 9 minutes or until lightly browned. Cool 1 minute on cookie sheets. Remove to cooling racks; cool completely.
Makes about 4 dozen cookies

Mocha Crinkles

Crispy Oat Drops

- 1 cup (2 sticks) butter or margarine, softened
- ½ cup granulated sugar
- ½ cup firmly packed light brown sugar
- 1 large egg
- 2 cups all-purpose flour
- ½ cup quick-cooking or old-fashioned oats, uncooked
- 1 teaspoon cream of tartar
- ½ teaspoon baking soda
- ¼ teaspoon salt
- 1¾ cups "M&M's"® Semi-Sweet Chocolate Mini Baking Bits
- 1 cup toasted rice cereal
- ½ cup shredded coconut
- ½ cup coarsely chopped pecans

Preheat oven to 350°F. In large bowl cream butter and sugars until light and fluffy; beat in egg. In medium bowl combine flour, oats, cream of tartar, baking soda and salt; blend flour mixture into creamed mixture. Stir in "M&M's"® Semi-Sweet Chocolate Mini Baking Bits, cereal, coconut and pecans. Drop by heaping tablespoonfuls about 2 inches apart onto ungreased cookie sheets. Bake 10 to 13 minutes or until lightly browned. Cool completely on wire racks. Store in tightly covered container.

Makes about 4 dozen cookies

Cocoa Nut Bundles

- 1 can (8 ounces) refrigerated quick crescent dinner rolls
- 2 tablespoons butter or margarine, softened
- 1 tablespoon granulated sugar
- 2 teaspoons HERSHEY'S® Cocoa
- ¼ cup chopped nuts
  Powdered sugar

1. Heat oven to 375°F. On ungreased cookie sheet, unroll dough and separate to form 8 triangles.

2. Combine butter, granulated sugar and cocoa. Add nuts; mix well. Divide mixture evenly among triangles, placing on wide ends. Take dough on either side of mixture and pull up and over mixture, tucking ends under. Continue rolling dough toward opposite point.

3. Bake 9 minutes or until golden brown. Sprinkle with powdered sugar. *Makes 8 rolls*

Crispy Oat Drops

Frosty's Colorful Cookies

- 1¼ cups firmly packed light brown sugar
- ¾ Butter Flavor* CRISCO® Stick or ¾ cup Butter Flavor* CRISCO all-vegetable shortening
- 2 tablespoons milk
- 1 tablespoon vanilla
- 1 egg
- 1¾ cups all-purpose flour
- 1 teaspoon salt
- ¾ teaspoon baking soda
- 2 cups red and green candy-coated chocolate pieces

*Butter Flavor Crisco® is artificially flavored.

1. Heat oven to 375°F. Place sheets of foil on countertop for cooling cookies.

2. Place brown sugar, ¾ cup shortening, milk and vanilla in large bowl. Beat at medium speed of electric mixer until well blended. Add egg; beat well.

3. Combine flour, salt and baking soda. Add to shortening mixture; beat at low speed just until blended. Stir in candy-coated chocolate pieces.

4. Drop dough by rounded measuring tablespoonfuls 3 inches apart onto ungreased baking sheets.

5. Bake one baking sheet at a time at 375°F for 8 to 10 minutes for chewy cookies, or 11 to 13 minutes for crisp cookies. *Do not overbake.* Cool 2 minutes on baking sheet. Remove cookies to foil to cool completely.

Makes about 3 dozen cookies

Hershey's Great American Chocolate Chip Cookies

- 1 cup (2 sticks) butter, softened
- ¾ cup granulated sugar
- ¾ cup packed light brown sugar
- 1 teaspoon vanilla extract
- 2 eggs
- 2¼ cups all-purpose flour
- 1 teaspoon baking soda
- ½ teaspoon salt
- 2 cups (12-ounce package) HERSHEY'S Semi-Sweet Chocolate Chips
- 1 cup chopped nuts (optional)

Heat oven to 375°F. In large mixer bowl, beat butter, granulated sugar, brown sugar and vanilla until creamy. Add eggs; beat well. Stir together flour, baking soda and salt; gradually add to butter mixture, beating well. Stir in chocolate chips and nuts, if desired. Drop dough by rounded teaspoonfuls onto ungreased cookie sheet. Bake 8 to 10 minutes or until lightly browned. Cool slightly; remove from cookie sheet to wire rack. Cool completely.

Makes about 6 dozen cookies

Hershey₀s Great American Chocolate Chip Pan Cookies: Spread dough into greased 15½×10½×1-inch jelly-roll pan. Bake at 375°F for 20 minutes or until lightly browned. Cool completely in pan on wire rack. Cut into bars. Makes about 4 dozen bars.

Skor® & Chocolate Chip Cookies: Omit 1 cup HERSHEY₀S Semi-Sweet Chocolate Chips and nuts; replace with 1 cup finely chopped SKOR® bars. Drop onto cookie sheets and bake as directed.

Great American Ice Cream Sandwiches: Prepare cookies as directed. Place one small scoop slightly softened vanilla ice cream between flat sides of two cookies. Gently press together. Wrap and freeze.

Cherry Cashew Cookies

1 cup butter or margarine, softened
¾ cup granulated sugar
¾ cup packed brown sugar
1 teaspoon vanilla extract
2 eggs
2¼ cups all-purpose flour
1 teaspoon baking soda
1 package (10 ounces) vanilla milk chips (about 1⅔ cups)
1 cup broken, salted cashews
1½ cups dried tart cherries

Preheat oven to 375°F.

In large mixer bowl, combine butter, granulated sugar, brown sugar, vanilla and eggs. Mix with electric mixer on medium speed until thoroughly combined. Combine flour and baking soda; gradually add flour mixture to butter mixture. Stir in vanilla milk chips, cashews and dried cherries. Drop by rounded tablespoonfuls onto ungreased baking sheets.

Bake 12 to 15 minutes or until light golden brown. Cool on wire racks and store in airtight container.

Makes 4½ dozen cookies

Favorite recipe from **Cherry Marketing Institute, Inc.**

Almond Milk Chocolate Chippers

½ **cup slivered almonds**
1¼ **cups all-purpose flour**
½ **teaspoon baking soda**
½ **teaspoon salt**
½ **cup butter or margarine, softened**
½ **cup firmly packed light brown sugar**
⅓ **cup granulated sugar**
1 **large egg**
2 **tablespoons almond-flavored liqueur**
1 **cup milk chocolate chips**

1. Preheat oven to 350°F. To toast almonds, spread on baking sheet. Bake 8 to 10 minutes or until golden brown, stirring frequently. Remove almonds from pan and cool; set aside.

2. Increase oven temperature to 375°F.

3. Place flour, baking soda and salt in small bowl; stir to combine.

4. Beat butter, brown sugar and granulated sugar in large bowl with electric mixer at medium speed until light and fluffy. Beat in egg until well blended. Beat in liqueur. Gradually add flour mixture. Beat at low speed until well blended. Stir in chips and almonds with mixing spoon.

5. Drop rounded teaspoonfuls of dough 2 inches apart onto ungreased cookie sheets.

6. Bake 9 to 10 minutes or until edges are golden brown. Let cookies stand on cookie sheets 2 minutes. Remove cookies with spatula to wire racks; cool completely.

7. Store tightly covered at room temperature or freeze up to 3 months.

Makes about 3 dozen cookies

Helpful Hint

Use shiny cookie sheets for the best cookie baking results. Dark cookie sheets can cause the bottoms of the cookies to be dark.

Almond Milk Chocolate Chippers

Maple Walnut Meringues

⅓ **cup powdered sugar**
½ **cup plus ⅓ cup ground walnuts, divided**
¾ **cup packed light brown sugar**
3 **egg whites, at room temperature**
   Pinch salt
⅛ **teaspoon cream of tartar**
1 **teaspoon maple extract**

Place 1 oven rack in the top third of oven and 1 oven rack in the bottom third of oven; preheat oven to 300°F. Line 2 large cookie sheets with aluminum foil, shiny side up.

Stir powdered sugar and ½ cup walnuts with fork in medium bowl; set aside. Crumble brown sugar into small bowl; set aside.

Beat egg whites and salt in large bowl with electric mixer at high speed until foamy. Add cream of tartar; beat 30 seconds or until mixture forms soft peaks. Sprinkle brown sugar 1 tablespoon at a time over egg white mixture; beat at high speed until each addition is completely absorbed. Beat 2 to 3 minutes or until mixture forms stiff peaks. Beat in maple extract at low speed. Fold in walnut mixture with large rubber spatula.

Drop level tablespoonfuls of dough to form mounds about 1 inch apart on prepared cookie sheets. Sprinkle cookies with remaining ⅓ cup ground walnuts. Bake 25 minutes or until cookies feel dry on surface but remain soft inside. (Rotate cookie sheets from top to bottom halfway through baking time.)

Slide foil with cookies onto wire racks; cool completely. Carefully remove cookies from foil. Store in airtight container with wax paper between layers of cookies. Cookies are best the day they are baked.

Makes about 36 cookies

Helpful Hint

Nuts can be ground easily in the food processor. Use the metal blade and process with quick on/off pulses until nuts are the desired texture.

Maple Walnut Meringues

Basic Banana Holiday Cookies

2¾ cups all-purpose flour
1 teaspoon baking soda
¼ teaspoon salt
1 cup margarine, softened
1¼ cups granulated sugar, divided
¼ cup packed brown sugar
1 egg
1 large, ripe DOLE® Banana, mashed (about ½ cup)
½ teaspoon ground cinnamon

• **Combine** flour, baking soda and salt in medium bowl; set aside.

• **Beat** together margarine, 1 cup granulated sugar and brown sugar in large bowl until creamy. Beat in egg and banana until blended. Stir in flour mixture until combined. Cover and chill 2 hours or overnight until dough is firm enough to handle.

• **Combine** remaining ¼ cup granulated sugar and cinnamon in small bowl.

• **Shape** dough into 1-inch balls. Roll in cinnamon mixture; place two inches apart on ungreased baking sheets.

• **Bake** at 350°F 10 to 12 minutes or until lightly browned. Carefully remove cookies to wire rack to cool completely.

Makes 4½ dozen

Chocolate Banana Stars: Prepare, shape and bake dough as directed except roll dough in 1 cup finely chopped DOLE® Almonds instead of cinnamon mixture. Immediately after baking, press unwrapped individual milk chocolate pieces into center of each cookie. Cool as directed.

Banana Chippers: Prepare and shape dough as directed except stir in 1 package (10 ounces) peanut butter chips and 1 cup chopped pecans or walnuts into dough and omit cinnamon mixture. Bake and cool as directed.

Zana Kringles: Stir 1 teaspoon ground ginger into flour mixture and replace brown sugar with 2 tablespoons molasses. Prepare, shape, bake and cool as directed.

Prep Time: 15 minutes
Bake Time: 12 minutes

Peanut Butter Crackles

1½ cups all-purpose flour
1 teaspoon baking soda
⅛ teaspoon salt
½ cup (1 stick) MAZOLA®
    Margarine, softened
½ cup SKIPPY® Creamy or
    SUPER CHUNK® Peanut
    Butter
½ cup granulated sugar
½ cup packed brown sugar
1 egg
1 teaspoon vanilla
    Granulated sugar
    Chocolate candy kisses

1. Preheat oven at 375°F. In small bowl, combine flour, baking soda and salt; set aside.

2. In large bowl, beat margarine and peanut butter until smooth. Beat in sugars until blended. Beat in egg and vanilla. Gradually beat in flour mixture until well mixed.

3. Shape dough into 1-inch balls. Roll in granulated sugar. Place 2 inches apart on ungreased cookie sheets.

4. Bake 10 minutes or until lightly browned. Remove from oven and quickly press chocolate candy kiss firmly into top of each cookie (cookie will crack around edges). Remove to wire racks to cool.
Makes about 5 dozen cookies

Molasses Spice Cookies

1 cup granulated sugar
¾ cup shortening
¼ cup molasses
1 large egg, beaten
2 cups all-purpose flour
2 teaspoons baking soda
1 teaspoon ground
    cinnamon
1 teaspoon ground cloves
1 teaspoon ground ginger
¼ teaspoon dry mustard
¼ teaspoon salt
½ cup granulated brown
    sugar

1. Preheat oven to 375°F. Grease cookie sheets. Beat granulated sugar and shortening about 5 minutes in large bowl until light and fluffy. Add molasses and egg; beat until fluffy.

2. Combine flour, baking soda, cinnamon, cloves, ginger, mustard and salt. Add to shortening mixture; mix until just combined.

3. Place brown sugar in shallow dish. Roll tablespoonfuls of dough into 1-inch balls; roll in sugar. Place on prepared cookie sheets. Bake 15 minutes or until lightly browned. Let stand on cookie sheets 2 minutes. Remove cookies to wire racks; cool completely.
Makes about 6 dozen cookies

Oatmeal Raisin Cookies

- ¾ **cup all-purpose flour**
- ¾ **teaspoon salt**
- ½ **teaspoon baking soda**
- ½ **teaspoon ground cinnamon**
- ¾ **cup butter or margarine, softened**
- ¾ **cup granulated sugar**
- ¾ **cup packed light brown sugar**
- 1 **egg**
- 1 **tablespoon water**
- 3 **teaspoons vanilla, divided**
- 3 **cups uncooked quick-cooking or old-fashioned oats**
- 1 **cup raisins**
- ½ **cup powdered sugar**
- 1 **tablespoon milk**

Preheat oven to 375°F. Grease cookie sheets; set aside. Combine flour, salt, baking soda and cinnamon in small bowl.

Beat butter, granulated sugar and brown sugar in large bowl with electric mixer at medium speed until light and fluffy. Add egg, water and 2 teaspoons vanilla; beat well. Add flour mixture; beat at low speed just until blended. Stir in oats with spoon. Stir in raisins.

Drop tablespoonfuls of dough 2 inches apart onto prepared cookie sheets.

Bake 10 to 11 minutes or until edges are golden brown. Let cookies stand 2 minutes on cookie sheets; transfer to wire racks to cool completely.

For glaze, stir powdered sugar, milk and remaining 1 teaspoon vanilla in small bowl until smooth. Drizzle over cookies with fork or spoon. Store cookies tightly covered at room temperature or freeze up to 3 months.

Makes about 48 cookies

Helpful Hint

Quick-cooking rolled oats and old-fashioned rolled oats are essentially the same; the quick-cooking oats simply cook faster because they have been rolled into thinner flakes.

Oatmeal Raisin Cookies

Chocolate Bonanza

Festive Fudge Blossoms

1 box (18.25 ounces) chocolate fudge cake
   mix
¼ cup butter or margarine, softened
1 egg, slightly beaten
¾ to 1 cup finely chopped walnuts
48 chocolate star candies

1. Preheat oven to 350°F. Cut butter into cake
mix in large bowl until mixture resembles coarse
crumbs. Stir in egg and 2 tablespoons water
until well blended.

2. Shape dough into ½-inch balls; roll in walnuts,
pressing nuts gently into dough. Place about
2 inches apart onto ungreased baking sheets.

continued on page 36

Festive Fudge Blossoms, continued

3. Bake cookies 12 minutes or until puffed and nearly set. Place chocolate star in center of each cookie; bake 1 minute more. Cool 2 minutes on baking sheet. Remove cookies from baking sheets to wire rack to cool completely.

Makes 4 dozen cookies

Prep and Bake Time: 30 minutes

Czech Bear Paws

4 cups toasted ground hazelnuts
2 cups all-purpose flour
1 tablespoon unsweetened cocoa powder
1 teaspoon ground cinnamon
½ teaspoon ground nutmeg
¼ teaspoon salt
1 cup plus 3 teaspoons butter, softened, divided
1 cup powdered sugar
1 large egg yolk
½ cup melted chocolate chips
Slivered almonds, halved

1. Preheat oven to 350°F. Place hazelnuts, flour, cocoa, cinnamon, nutmeg and salt in medium bowl; stir to combine.

2. Beat 1 cup butter, powdered sugar and egg yolk in large bowl with electric mixer at medium speed until light and fluffy. Gradually add flour mixture. Beat at low speed until soft dough forms.

3. Grease 3 madeleine pans with remaining butter, 1 teaspoon per pan; dust with flour. (If only 1 madeleine pan is available, thoroughly wash, dry, regrease and flour after baking each batch. Cover remaining dough with plastic wrap; let stand at room temperature.) Press level tablespoonfuls of dough into each mold.

4. Bake 12 minutes or until lightly browned. Let cookies stand in pan 3 minutes. Carefully loosen cookies from pan with point of small knife. Invert pan over wire racks; tap lightly to release cookies. Let stand 2 minutes. Turn cookies shell-side up; cool completely.

5. Pipe squiggle of melted chocolate on curved end of each cookie; place slivered almond halves in melted chocolate for claws. Let stand at room temperature 1 hour or until set.

6. Store tightly covered at room temperature. These cookies do not freeze well.

Makes about 5 dozen cookies

Czech Bear Paws

S'more Snack Treats

44 squares HONEY MAID®
Honey Grahams
(2 sleeves)
3 tablespoons margarine
1 (10-ounce) package
marshmallows
¾ cup miniature semisweet
chocolate chips

1. Break grahams into bite-size pieces; set aside.

2. Heat margarine in large saucepan over medium heat until melted. Add marshmallows, stirring constantly until melted.

3. Stir broken crackers into marshmallow mixture to coat evenly. Spread mixture into lightly greased 13×9×2-inch pan; sprinkle with chocolate chips, pressing lightly with greased hands.

4. Chill at least 20 minutes before cutting into squares.

Makes 12 s'mores

Preparation Time: 15 minutes
Cook Time: 20 minutes
Chill Time: 20 minutes
Total Time: 55 minutes

Triple Chocolate Cookies

1 package DUNCAN HINES®
Moist Deluxe® Swiss
Chocolate Cake Mix
½ cup butter or margarine,
melted
1 egg
½ cup semi-sweet chocolate
chips
½ cup milk chocolate chips
½ cup coarsely chopped
white chocolate
½ cup chopped pecans

1. Preheat oven to 375°F.

2. Combine cake mix, melted butter and egg in large bowl. Beat at low speed with electric mixer until blended. Stir in all 3 chocolates and pecans.

3. Drop by rounded tablespoonfuls onto ungreased baking sheets. Bake at 375°F 9 to 11 minutes. Cool 1 minute on baking sheet. Remove to cooling racks.

Makes 3½ to 4 dozen
cookies

Tip: Cookies may be stored in an airtight container in freezer for up to 6 months.

S'more Snack Treats

Chocolate Sugar Spritz

**2 squares (1 ounce each)
    unsweetened chocolate,
    coarsely chopped**
2¼ cups all-purpose flour
¼ teaspoon salt
**1 cup butter or margarine,
    softened**
¾ cup granulated sugar
1 large egg
1 teaspoon almond extract
½ cup powdered sugar
**1 teaspoon ground
    cinnamon**

1. Preheat oven to 400°F.

2. Melt chocolate in small, heavy saucepan over low heat, stirring constantly; set aside.

3. Combine flour and salt in small bowl; stir to combine.

4. Beat butter and granulated sugar in large bowl with electric mixer at medium speed until light and fluffy, scraping down side of bowl once. Beat in egg and almond extract, scraping down side of bowl. Beat in chocolate. Gradually add flour mixture with mixing spoon. (Dough will be stiff.)

5. Fit cookie press with desired plate (or change plates for different shapes after first batch). Fill press with dough; press dough 1 inch apart onto ungreased cookie sheets.

6. Bake 7 minutes or until just set.

7. Combine powdered sugar and cinnamon in small bowl. Transfer to fine-mesh strainer and sprinkle over hot cookies while they are still on cookie sheets. Remove cookies with spatula to wire racks; cool completely.

8. Store tightly covered at room temperature. These cookies do not freeze well.
    Makes 4 to 5 dozen cookies

Tip: Cool baking sheet completely before baking each batch of cookies.

Triple Chocolate Pretzels

**½ cup butter or margarine,
    softened**
½ cup granulated sugar
1 egg
**2 squares (1 ounce each)
    unsweetened chocolate,
    melted and cooled**
2 cups cake flour
1 teaspoon vanilla
¼ teaspoon salt
    **Mocha Glaze (recipe
    follows)**
**2 ounces white chocolate,
    melted**

Cream butter and granulated sugar in large bowl until light. Add egg and melted chocolate; beat until fluffy. Stir in cake flour, vanilla and salt until well blended. Cover; refrigerate until firm, about 1 hour.

Preheat oven to 400°F. Lightly grease cookie sheets or line with parchment paper. Divide dough into 4 equal parts. Divide each part into 12 pieces. Knead each piece briefly to soften dough. Roll into a rope about 6 inches long. Form into pretzel shape on prepared cookie sheet. Repeat with all pieces of dough, spacing cookies 2 inches apart. Bake 7 to 9 minutes or until firm. Remove to wire racks to cool. Prepare Mocha Glaze. Dip pretzels, one at a time, into glaze to coat completely. Place on waxed paper, right side up. Let stand until glaze is set. Squeeze melted white chocolate through pastry bag or drizzle over pretzels. Let stand until chocolate is completely set.

Makes 4 dozen cookies

Mocha Glaze: Heat 1 cup semisweet chocolate chips, 1 teaspoon light corn syrup and 1 teaspoon shortening in small saucepan over low heat until chocolate is melted. Stir in 1 cup powdered sugar and 3 to 5 tablespoons hot coffee or water until glaze is smooth.

Festive Chocolate Chip Cookies

1 package **DUNCAN HINES®
    Moist Deluxe® White
    Cake Mix**
¼ cup firmly packed light
    brown sugar
1 egg
¾ cup vegetable oil
1 package (6 ounces) semi-
    sweet chocolate chips
½ cup chopped pecans or
    walnuts
    Assorted decors

1. Preheat oven to 350°F.

2. Combine cake mix, brown sugar, egg and oil in large bowl. Beat at low speed with electric mixer until blended. Stir in chocolate chips and pecans. Form dough into 1½-inch ball. Dip top of ball in decors. Place ball decor-side up on ungreased baking sheets. Repeat with remaining dough, placing balls 2 inches apart on baking sheets. Bake at 350°F 10 to 12 minutes or until light golden brown around edges. Cool 2 minutes on baking sheets. Remove to cooling racks. Cool completely. Store in airtight container.

*Makes 3 to 3½ dozen
cookies*

Chocolate Peanut Butter Cup Cookies

Cookies

- **1 cup semi-sweet chocolate chips**
- **2 squares (1 ounce each) unsweetened baking chocolate**
- **1 cup sugar**
- **½ Butter Flavor* CRISCO® Stick or ½ cup Butter Flavor* CRISCO® all-vegetable shortening**
- **2 eggs**
- **1 teaspoon salt**
- **1 teaspoon vanilla**
- **1½ cups plus 2 tablespoons all-purpose flour**
- **½ teaspoon baking soda**
- **¾ cup finely chopped peanuts**
- **36 miniature peanut butter cups, unwrapped**

Drizzle

- **1 cup peanut butter chips**

*Butter Flavor Crisco® is artificially flavored.

1. Heat oven to 350°F. Place sheets of foil on countertop for cooling cookies.

2. For cookies, combine chocolate chips and chocolate squares in microwave-safe measuring cup or bowl. Microwave at 50% (MEDIUM). Stir after 2 minutes. Repeat until smooth (or melt on rangetop in small saucepan on very low heat). Cool slightly.

3. Combine sugar and ½ cup shortening in large bowl. Beat at medium speed of electric mixer until blended and crumbly. Beat in eggs, one at a time, then salt and vanilla. Reduce speed to low. Add chocolate slowly. Mix until well blended. Stir in flour and baking soda with spoon until well blended. Shape dough into 1¼-inch balls. Roll in nuts. Place 2 inches apart on ungreased baking sheet.

4. Bake at 350°F for 8 to 10 minutes or until set. *Do not overbake.* Press peanut butter cup into center of each cookie immediately. Press cookie against cup. Cool 2 minutes on baking sheet before removing to cooling rack. Cool completely.

5. For drizzle, place peanut butter chips in heavy resealable sandwich bag. Seal. Microwave at 50% (MEDIUM). Knead bag after 1 minute. Repeat until smooth (or melt by placing bag in hot water). Cut tiny tip off corner of bag. Squeeze out and drizzle over cookies.

Makes 3 dozen cookies

Chocolate Peanut Butter Cup Cookies

Nutty Clusters

2 squares (1 ounce each)
   unsweetened chocolate
½ cup butter or margarine,
   softened
1 cup granulated sugar
1 egg
⅓ cup buttermilk
1 teaspoon vanilla
1¾ cups all-purpose flour
½ teaspoon baking soda
1 cup mixed salted nuts,
   coarsely chopped
   Easy Chocolate Icing
   (recipe follows)

Preheat oven to 400°F. Line cookie sheets with parchment paper or leave ungreased.

Melt chocolate in top of double boiler over hot, not boiling, water. Remove from heat; cool. Beat butter and granulated sugar in large bowl until smooth. Beat in egg, melted chocolate, buttermilk and vanilla until light. Stir in flour, baking soda and nuts. Drop dough by teaspoonfuls 2 inches apart onto cookie sheets.

Bake 8 to 10 minutes or until almost no imprint remains when touched. Immediately remove cookies from cookie sheets to wire racks. While cookies bake,

prepare Easy Chocolate Icing. Frost cookies while still warm.

Makes about 4 dozen cookies

Easy Chocolate Icing

2 squares (1 ounce each)
   unsweetened chocolate
2 tablespoons butter or
   margarine
2 cups powdered sugar
2 to 3 tablespoons water

Melt chocolate and butter in small heavy saucepan over low heat, stirring until completely melted. Add powdered sugar and water, mixing until smooth.

Helpful Hint

Parchment paper makes kitchen cleanup a breeze. It is available at gourmet kitchenware stores and at many supermarkets.

Nutty Clusters

Chewy Brownie Cookies

1½ cups firmly packed light
    brown sugar
⅔ CRISCO® Stick or ⅔ cup
    CRISCO® all-vegetable
    shortening
1 tablespoon water
1 teaspoon vanilla
2 eggs
1½ cups all-purpose flour
⅓ cup unsweetened baking
    cocoa
½ teaspoon salt
¼ teaspoon baking soda
2 cups semi-sweet chocolate
    chips (12-ounce
    package)

1. Heat oven to 375°F. Place
sheets of foil on countertop for
cooling cookies.

2. Combine brown sugar,
shortening, water and vanilla in
large bowl. Beat at medium speed
of electric mixer until well blended.
Beat eggs into creamed mixture.

3. Combine flour, cocoa, salt and
baking soda. Mix into creamed
mixture at low speed just until
blended. Stir in chocolate chips.

4. Drop rounded measuring
tablespoonfuls of dough 2 inches
apart onto ungreased baking
sheet.

5. Bake one baking sheet at a
time at 375°F for 7 to 9 minutes,
or until cookies are set. *Do not
overbake.* Cool 2 minutes on
baking sheet. Remove cookies
to foil to cool completely.

*Makes about 3 dozen
cookies*

Swiss Mocha Treats

2 ounces imported Swiss
    bittersweet chocolate
    candy bar, broken
½ cup plus 2 tablespoons
    butter, softened and
    divided
1 tablespoon instant
    espresso powder
1 teaspoon vanilla
1¾ cups all-purpose flour
½ teaspoon baking soda
½ teaspoon salt
¾ cup sugar
1 large egg
3 ounces imported Swiss
    white chocolate candy
    bar, broken

Melt bittersweet chocolate and 2
tablespoons butter in small, heavy
saucepan over low heat, stirring
often. Add espresso powder; stir
until dissolved. Remove mixture
from heat; stir in vanilla. Let cool
to room temperature.

Place flour, baking soda and salt in medium bowl; stir to combine. Beat ½ cup butter and sugar in large bowl with electric mixer at medium speed until light and fluffy. Beat in chocolate mixture and egg. Gradually add flour mixture. Beat at low speed until well blended. Cover; refrigerate 30 minutes or until firm.

Preheat oven to 375°F. Roll tablespoonfuls of dough into 1-inch balls. Place balls 3 inches apart on ungreased cookie sheets. Flatten each ball into ½-inch-thick round with fork dipped in sugar. Bake 9 to 10 minutes or until set (do not overbake or cookies will become dry). Immediately remove cookies to wire racks; cool completely.

Place white chocolate in small resealable plastic freezer bag; seal bag. Microwave at MEDIUM (50% power) 1 minute. Turn bag over; microwave at MEDIUM 1 minute or until melted. Knead bag until chocolate is smooth. Cut off very tiny corner of bag; pipe or drizzle white chocolate decoratively onto cooled cookies. Let stand at room temperature 30 minutes or until set. Store tightly covered at room temperature or freeze up to 3 months.

Makes about 4 dozen cookies

Chocolate Macaroons

1 can (8 ounces) almond paste
½ cup powdered sugar
2 egg whites
12 ounces semisweet baking chocolate or chips, melted
2 tablespoons all-purpose flour
Powdered sugar (optional)

Preheat oven to 300°F. Line cookie sheets with parchment paper; set aside.

Beat almond paste, ½ cup sugar and egg whites in large bowl with electric mixer at medium speed for 1 minute, scraping down side of bowl once. Beat in chocolate until well combined. Beat in flour at low speed, scraping down side of bowl once.

Spoon dough into pastry bag fitted with rosette tip. Pipe 1½-inch spirals 1 inch apart onto prepared cookie sheets. Pipe all cookies at once; dough will get stiff upon standing.

Bake 20 minutes or until set. Carefully remove parchment paper to countertop; cool completely.

Peel cookies off parchment paper. Sprinkle powdered sugar over cookies, if desired.

Makes about 3 dozen cookies

Double Chocolate Walnut Drops

¾ cup (1½ sticks) butter or
   margarine, softened
¾ cup granulated sugar
¾ cup firmly packed light
   brown sugar
1 large egg
1 teaspoon vanilla extract
2¼ cups all-purpose flour
⅓ cup unsweetened cocoa
   powder
1 teaspoon baking soda
½ teaspoon salt
1¾ cups "M&M's"® Chocolate
   Mini Baking Bits
1 cup coarsely chopped
   English or black walnuts

Preheat oven to 350°F. Lightly grease cookie sheets; set aside. In large bowl cream butter and sugars until light and fluffy; beat in egg and vanilla. In medium bowl combine flour, cocoa powder, baking soda and salt; add to creamed mixture. Stir in "M&M's"® Chocolate Mini Baking Bits and nuts. Drop by heaping tablespoonfuls about 2 inches apart onto prepared cookie sheets. Bake 12 to 14 minutes for chewy cookies or 14 to 16 minutes for crispy cookies. Cool completely on wire racks. Store in tightly covered container.

Makes about 4 dozen cookies

Variation: Shape dough into 2-inch-thick roll. Cover with plastic wrap; refrigerate. When ready to bake, slice dough into ¼-inch-thick slices and bake as directed.

Helpful Hint

Holiday gifts from the kitchen are always appreciated. It's nice to pair your gifts of food with complementary items, such as a set of oven mitts with a tin of Christmas cookies, or a cake server with your favorite cake.

Double Chocolate Walnut Drops

Holiday Favorites

Candy Cane Cookies

  1 cup sugar
  ⅔ cup margarine, softened
  ½ cup egg substitute
  2 teaspoons vanilla extract
  1 teaspoon almond extract
  3 cups all-purpose flour
  1 teaspoon DAVIS® Baking Powder
  ½ teaspoon red food coloring

1. Beat sugar and margarine in large bowl with mixer at medium speed until creamy. Beat in egg substitute, vanilla and almond extracts.

2. Mix flour and baking powder in small bowl; stir into margarine mixture.

continued on page 52

50

Candy Cane Cookies, continued

3. Divide dough in half; tint half with red food coloring. Wrap each half and refrigerate at least 2 hours.

4. Divide each half into 32 pieces. Roll each piece into a 5-inch rope. Twist 1 red and 1 white rope together and bend 1 end to form candy cane shape. Place on ungreased baking sheets.

5. Bake in preheated 350°F oven for 8 to 10 minutes or just until set and lightly golden. Remove from sheets; cool on wire racks. Store in airtight container.

Makes 32 cookies

Preparation Time: 20 minutes
Chill Time: 2 hours
Cook Time: 8 minutes
Total Time: 2 hours and 28 minutes

Snowball Cookies

> 1 cup margarine or butter, softened
> 1 cup sugar
> 1 teaspoon vanilla extract
> 2 cups all-purpose flour
> 1½ cups PLANTERS® Pecans, finely ground
> ¼ teaspoon salt
> ½ cup powdered sugar

1. Beat margarine, sugar and vanilla in large bowl with mixer at medium speed until creamy. Blend in flour, pecans and salt. Refrigerate 1 hour.

2. Shape dough into 1-inch balls. Place on ungreased baking sheets, 2 inches apart. Bake in preheated 350°F oven for 10 to 12 minutes. Remove from sheets; cool on wire racks. Dust with powdered sugar. Store in airtight container. *Makes 6 dozen*

Preparation Time: 15 minutes
Chill Time: 1 hour
Cook Time: 10 minutes
Total Time: 1 hour and 25 minutes

Slice 'n' Bake Ginger Wafers

½ **cup butter or margarine, softened**
1 **cup packed brown sugar**
¼ **cup light molasses**
1 **egg**
2 **teaspoons ground ginger**
1 **teaspoon grated orange peel**
¼ **teaspoon salt**
¼ **teaspoon ground cinnamon**
¼ **teaspoon ground cloves**
2 **cups all-purpose flour**

1. Beat butter, sugar and molasses in large bowl until light and fluffy. Add egg, ginger, orange peel, salt, cinnamon and cloves; beat until well blended. Stir in flour until well blended. (Dough will be very stiff.)

2. Divide dough in half. Roll each half into 8×1½-inch log. Wrap logs in wax paper or plastic wrap; refrigerate at least 5 hours or up to 3 days.

3. Preheat oven to 350°F. Cut dough into ¼-inch-thick slices. Place about 2 inches apart onto ungreased baking sheets. Bake 12 to 14 minutes or until set. Remove from baking sheet to wire rack to cool.

Makes about 4½ dozen cookies

Serving Suggestion: Dip half of each cookie in melted white chocolate or drizzle cookies with a glaze of 1¼ cups powdered sugar and 2 tablespoons orange juice. Or, cut cookie dough into ⅛-inch-thick slices; bake and sandwich melted caramel candy or peanut butter between cookies.

Helpful Hint

One medium orange yields one to two tablespoons grated peel, which can be frozen for up to six months.

Slice 'n' Bake Ginger Wafers

Pumpkin White Chocolate Drops

2 cups butter or margarine, softened
2 cups granulated sugar
1 can (16 ounces) solid pack pumpkin
2 eggs
4 cups all-purpose flour
2 teaspoons pumpkin pie spice
1 teaspoon baking powder
½ teaspoon baking soda
1 bag (12 ounces) vanilla baking chips
1 container (16 ounces) ready-to-spread cream cheese frosting
¼ cup packed brown sugar

1. Preheat oven to 375°F. Grease cookie sheets. Beat butter and sugar in large bowl until light and fluffy. Add pumpkin and eggs; beat until smooth. Add flour, pumpkin pie spice, baking powder and baking soda; beat just until well blended. Stir in chips.

2. Drop dough by teaspoonfuls about 2 inches apart onto cookie sheets. Bake about 16 minutes or until set and bottoms are brown. Cool 1 minute on cookie sheets. Remove from cookie sheets to wire rack to cool.

3. Combine frosting and brown sugar in small bowl. Spread on warm cookies.

Makes about 6 dozen cookies

Jumbles

½ cup (1 stick) butter or margarine, softened
½ cup granulated sugar
¼ cup firmly packed light brown sugar
1 large egg
1¼ cups all-purpose flour
½ teaspoon baking soda
1¾ cups "M&M's"® Chocolate Mini Baking Bits
1 cup raisins
1 cup chopped walnuts

Preheat oven to 350°F. Lightly grease cookie sheets. Cream butter and sugars until light and fluffy; beat in egg. Combine flour and baking soda; blend into creamed mixture. Stir in remaining ingredients. Drop by rounded tablespoonfuls onto cookie sheets. Bake 13 to 15 minutes. Cool 2 to 3 minutes on cookie sheets; cool completely on wire racks.

Makes about 3 dozen cookies

Pumpkin White Chocolate Drops

Snowmen

1 package (20 ounces) refrigerated chocolate chip cookie dough
1½ cups sifted powdered sugar
2 tablespoons milk
Candy corn, gum drops, chocolate chips, licorice and other assorted small candies

1. Preheat oven to 375°F.

2. Cut dough into 12 equal sections. Divide each section into 3 balls: large, medium and small for each snowman.

3. For each snowman, place 3 balls in row, ¼ inch apart, on ungreased cookie sheet. Repeat with remaining dough.

4. Bake 10 to 12 minutes or until edges are very lightly browned.

5. Cool 4 minutes on cookie sheets. Remove to wire racks; cool completely.

6. Mix powdered sugar and milk in medium bowl until smooth. Pour over cookies. Let cookies stand 20 minutes or until set.

7. Decorate to create faces, hats and arms with assorted candies.
Makes 1 dozen cookies

Scrumptious Chocolate Fruit and Nut Cookies

1¼ cups butter or margarine, softened
2 cups sugar
2 eggs
2 teaspoons vanilla extract
2 cups all-purpose flour
¾ cup HERSHEY'S Cocoa
1 teaspoon baking soda
½ teaspoon salt
2 cups (12-ounce package) HERSHEY'S Semi-Sweet Chocolate Chips
1 cup chopped dried apricots
1 cup coarsely chopped macadamia nuts

Heat oven to 350°F.

In large mixer bowl beat butter and sugar until light and fluffy. Add eggs and vanilla; beat well. Stir together flour, cocoa, baking soda and salt; blend into butter mixture. Stir in chocolate chips, apricots and nuts. Using ice cream scoop or ¼ cup measuring cup, drop dough onto ungreased cookie sheet.

Bake 12 to 14 minutes or until set. Cool slightly; remove from cookie sheet to wire rack. Cool completely.
Makes about 2 dozen (3½-inch) cookies

Snowmen

Holiday Sugar Cookies

2 cups all-purpose flour
½ teaspoon baking soda
1 cup FLEISCHMANN'S®
 Original Margarine,
 softened
1 cup plus 2 tablespoons
 sugar, divided
1 teaspoon vanilla extract
¼ cup EGG BEATERS®
 Healthy Real Egg
 Substitute

1. Mix flour and baking soda in small bowl; set aside.

2. Beat margarine, 1 cup sugar and vanilla in large bowl with mixer at medium speed until creamy. Beat in egg substitute until light and fluffy. Gradually blend in flour mixture. Wrap; refrigerate 4 hours.

3. Shape rounded teaspoons of dough into balls using floured hands. Place 2 inches apart on ungreased baking sheets. Grease bottom of small glass; dip in remaining sugar. Press balls to flatten slightly, dipping glass in remaining sugar as necessary.

4. Bake in preheated 375°F oven for 8 to 10 minutes. Remove from sheets; cool completely on wire racks.   *Makes 4½ dozen*

Cherry Dot Cookies

2¼ cups all-purpose flour
2 teaspoons baking powder
½ teaspoon salt
¾ cup margarine, softened
1 cup sugar
2 eggs
2 tablespoons skim milk
1 teaspoon vanilla
1 cup chopped nuts
1 cup finely chopped pitted
 dates
⅓ cup finely chopped
 maraschino cherries
2⅔ cups KELLOGG'S® CORN
 FLAKES® cereal,
 crushed to 1⅓ cups
15 maraschino cherries, cut
 into quarters

1. Stir together flour, baking powder and salt. Set aside.

2. In large mixing bowl, beat margarine and sugar until light and fluffy. Add eggs. Beat well. Stir in milk and vanilla. Add flour mixture. Mix well. Stir in nuts, dates and the ⅓ cup cherries.

3. Shape level measuring-tablespoons of dough into balls. Roll in KELLOGG'S CORN FLAKES® cereal. Place on baking sheets coated with cooking spray. Top each with cherry quarter.

4. Bake at 350°F about 10 minutes or until lightly browned.
Makes 5 dozen cookies

Peanut Butter Treats

1¼ cups firmly packed light brown sugar
¾ Butter Flavor* CRISCO® stick or ¾ cup Butter Flavor* CRISCO® all-vegetable shortening
2 tablespoons milk
1 tablespoon vanilla
1 egg
1¾ cups all-purpose flour
1 teaspoon salt
¾ teaspoon baking soda
2 cups (about 32) miniature peanut butter cups, unwrapped and quartered or coarsely chopped

*Butter Flavor Crisco® is artificially flavored.

1. Heat oven to 375°F. Place sheets of foil on countertop for cooling cookies.

2. Place brown sugar, shortening, milk and vanilla in large bowl. Beat at medium speed of electric mixer until well blended. Add egg; beat well.

3. Combine flour, salt and baking soda. Add to shortening mixture; beat at low speed just until blended. Stir in peanut butter cup quarters.

4. Drop dough by rounded measuring tablespoonfuls 3 inches apart onto *ungreased* baking sheets.

5. Bake one baking sheet at a time at 375°F for 8 to 10 minutes or until cookies are lightly browned. *Do not overbake.* Cool 2 minutes on baking sheet. Remove cookies to foil to cool completely.
Makes about 3 dozen cookies

Helpful Hint

Hardened brown sugar can be softened quickly in the microwave. Place one cup sugar in a covered microwavable dish; heat at HIGH 30 to 60 seconds. Repeat if necessary.

Fruitcake Slices

1 cup butter or margarine, softened
1 cup powdered sugar
1 egg
1 teaspoon vanilla extract
1½ cups coarsely chopped candied fruit (fruitcake mix)
½ cup coarsely chopped walnuts
2½ cups all-purpose unsifted flour, divided
¾ to 1 cup flaked coconut

Beat butter in large bowl with electric mixer at medium speed until smooth. Add powdered sugar; beat until well blended. Add egg and vanilla; beat until well blended.

Combine candied fruit and walnuts in medium bowl. Stir ¼ cup flour into fruit mixture. Add remaining 2¼ cups flour to butter mixture; beat at low speed until blended. Stir in fruit mixture with spoon.

Shape dough into 2 logs, each about 2 inches in diameter and 5½ inches long. Spread coconut evenly on sheet of waxed paper. Roll logs in coconut, coating evenly. Wrap each log in plastic wrap. Refrigerate 2 to 3 hours or overnight, or freeze up to 1 month. (Let frozen logs stand at room temperature about 10 minutes before slicing and baking.)

Preheat oven to 350°F. Grease cookie sheets. Cut logs into ¼-inch-thick slices; place 1 inch apart on cookie sheets.

Bake 13 to 15 minutes or until edges are golden brown. Transfer to wire racks to cool. Store in airtight container.

Makes about 48 cookies

Helpful Hint

Make a double batch of dough to freeze if you have extra time before the holidays. These rolls of dough can be defrosted whenever you have unexpected guests or need a last-minute homemade gift.

Fruitcake Slices

Jolly Peanut Butter Gingerbread Cookies

1⅔ cups (10-ounce package) REESE'S®
   Peanut Butter Chips
¾ cup (1½ sticks) butter or margarine,
   softened
1 cup packed light brown sugar
1 cup dark corn syrup
2 eggs
5 cups all-purpose flour
1 teaspoon baking soda
½ teaspoon ground cinnamon
¼ teaspoon ground ginger
¼ teaspoon salt

1. Place peanut butter chips in small microwave-safe bowl. Microwave at HIGH (100%) 1 to

continued on page 68

66

Jolly Peanut Butter Gingerbread Cookies, continued

2 minutes or until chips are melted when stirred. In large bowl, beat melted peanut butter chips and butter until well blended. Add brown sugar, corn syrup and eggs; beat until light and fluffy. Stir together flour, baking soda, cinnamon, ginger and salt. Add half of flour mixture to butter mixture; beat on low speed of electric mixer until smooth. With wooden spoon, stir in remaining flour mixture until well blended. Divide into thirds; wrap each in plastic wrap. Refrigerate at least 1 hour or until dough is firm enough to roll.

2. Heat oven to 325°F.

3. Roll 1 dough portion at a time to ⅛-inch thickness on lightly floured surface; with floured cookie cutters, cut into holiday shapes. Place on ungreased cookie sheet.

4. Bake 10 to 12 minutes or until set and lightly browned. Cool slightly; remove from cookie sheet to wire rack. Cool completely. Frost and decorate as desired.

Makes about 6 dozen cookies

Butter Cookies

¾ **cup butter or margarine, softened**
¼ **cup granulated sugar**
¼ **cup packed light brown sugar**
1 **egg yolk**
1¾ **cups all-purpose flour**
¾ **teaspoon baking powder**
⅛ **teaspoon salt**

1. Combine butter, sugars and egg yolk in medium bowl. Add flour, baking powder and salt; mix well. Cover; refrigerate until firm, about 4 hours or overnight.

2. Preheat oven to 350°F.

3. Roll dough on lightly floured surface to ¼-inch thickness; cut into desired shapes with cookie cutters. Place on ungreased cookie sheets.

4. Bake 8 to 10 minutes or until edges begin to brown. Remove to wire racks; cool completely.

Makes about 2 dozen cookies

Gingerbread Cookies

¾ cup light or dark molasses
¾ cup margarine or butter
¾ cup packed light brown
    sugar
4½ cups all-purpose flour
1 tablespoon ground ginger
2 teaspoons ground
    cinnamon
1 teaspoon DAVIS® Baking
    Powder
½ teaspoon baking soda
½ teaspoon ground nutmeg
¼ cup egg substitute
    Decorator icing, raisins
    and assorted candies,
    optional

1. Heat molasses, margarine
or butter and brown sugar in
saucepan over medium heat to a
boil, stirring occasionally. Remove
from heat; cool.

2. Mix flour, ginger, cinnamon,
baking powder, baking soda and
nutmeg in large bowl. Blend egg
substitute into molasses mixture.
Stir molasses mixture into flour
mixture until smooth. Wrap dough;
refrigerate 1 hour.

3. Divide dough in half. Roll dough
to ¼-inch thickness on floured
surface. Cut with floured 5×3-inch
gingerbread man cutter. Place onto
lightly greased baking sheets.

4. Bake in preheated 350°F oven
for 10 to 12 minutes or until lightly
browned. Remove from sheets;
cool on wire racks. Decorate as
desired with icing, raisins and
candies.   *Makes 2 dozen*

Preparation Time: 30 minutes
Chill Time: 1 hour
Cook Time: 10 minutes
Total Time: 1 hour and 40 minutes

Helpful Hint

When rolling out
cookie dough, work with
small amounts at a time; keep
the remaining dough covered
with plastic wrap to prevent
drying out.

Christmas Tree Platter

**Christmas Ornament
Cookie Dough (recipe
follows)**
**2 cups sifted powdered
sugar**
**2 tablespoons milk or lemon
juice**
**Assorted food colors,
colored sugars and
assorted small decors**

1. Preheat oven to 350°F. Prepare Christmas Ornament Cookie Dough. Divide dough in half. Reserve 1 half; refrigerate remaining dough. Roll reserved half of dough to ⅛-inch thickness.

2. Cut out tree shapes with cookie cutters. Place on ungreased cookie sheets.

3. Bake 10 to 12 minutes or until edges are lightly browned. Remove to wire racks; cool completely.

4. Repeat with remaining half of dough. Reroll scraps; cut into small circles for ornaments, squares and rectangles for gift boxes and tree trunks.

5. Bake 8 to 12 minutes, depending on size of cookies.

6. Mix sugar and milk for icing. Tint most of icing green and a smaller amount red or other colors for ornaments and boxes. Spread green icing on trees. Sprinkle ornaments and boxes with colored sugars or decorate as desired.

7. Arrange cookies on flat platter to resemble tree as shown in photo. *Makes about 1 dozen cookies*

Christmas Ornament Cookie Dough

2¼ cups all-purpose flour
¼ teaspoon salt
1 cup granulated sugar
**¾ cup butter or margarine,
softened**
1 egg
1 teaspoon vanilla
1 teaspoon almond extract

Combine flour and salt in medium bowl. Beat sugar and butter in large bowl at medium speed of electric mixer until fluffy. Beat in egg, vanilla and almond extract. Gradually add flour mixture. Beat at low speed until well blended. Form dough into 2 discs; wrap in plastic wrap and refrigerate 30 minutes or until firm.

Christmas Tree Platter

Stained Glass Cookies

½ **cup margarine or butter, softened**
½ **cup sugar**
½ **cup honey**
¼ **cup egg substitute**
1 **teaspoon vanilla extract**
3 **cups all-purpose flour**
1 **teaspoon DAVIS® Baking Powder**
½ **teaspoon baking soda**
½ **teaspoon salt**
5 **(.90-ounce) rolls Five Flavor or Fancy Fruits LIFE SAVERS® Candy**

1. Beat together margarine or butter, sugar, honey, egg substitute and vanilla in bowl with mixer until creamy. Mix in flour, baking powder, baking soda and salt. Cover; refrigerate at least 2 hours.

2. Roll dough on a lightly floured surface to ¼-inch thickness. Cut dough into desired shapes with 2½- to 3-inch floured cookie cutters. Trace a smaller version of cookie shape on dough leaving a ½- to ¾-inch border of dough. Cut out and remove dough from center of cookies; set aside. Place cut-out shapes on baking sheets lined with foil. Repeat with reserved dough, re-rolling scraps as necessary.

3. Crush each color of candy separately between two layers of wax paper. Spoon crushed candy inside centers of cut-out cookie shapes.

4. Bake in preheated 350°F oven for 6 to 8 minutes or until candy is melted and cookies are lightly browned. Cool cookies completely before removing from foil.

Makes 3½ dozen cookies

Preparation Time: 1 hour
Chill Time: 2 hours
Cook Time: 6 minutes
Total Time: 3 hours and 6 minutes

Helpful Hint

If your honey has crystallized, remove the lid and place the jar or bottle in the microwave. Microwave at HIGH 15 to 40 seconds (time varies with the amount of honey in the container).

Stained Glass Cookies

Christmas Cookie Pops

**1 package (20 ounces)
    refrigerated sugar
    cookie dough
All-purpose flour (optional)
20 to 24 (4-inch) lollipop sticks
Royal Icing (page 77)
6 ounces almond bark
    (vanilla or chocolate), or
    butterscotch chips
Vegetable shortening
Assorted small candies**

1. Preheat oven to 350°F. Grease cookie sheets; set aside.

2. Remove dough from wrapper according to package directions.

3. Sprinkle dough with flour to minimize sticking, if necessary. Cut dough in half. Reserve 1 half; refrigerate remaining dough.

4. Roll reserved dough to ⅓-inch thickness. Cut out cookies using 3¼- or 3½-inch Christmas cookie cutters. Place lollipop sticks on cookies so that tips of sticks are imbedded in cookies. Carefully turn cookies with spatula so sticks are in back; place on prepared cookie sheets. Repeat with remaining dough.

5. Bake 7 to 11 minutes or until edges are lightly browned. Cool cookies on sheets 2 minutes. Remove cookies to wire racks; cool completely.

6. Prepare Royal Icing.

7. Melt almond bark in medium microwavable bowl according to package directions. Add 1 or more tablespoons shortening if coating is too thick. Hold cookies over bowl; spoon coating over cookies. Scrape excess coating from cookie edges. Decorate with small candies and Royal Icing immediately. Place cookies on wire racks set over waxed paper; let harden. Store in tin at room temperature.

Makes 20 to 24 cookies

Helpful Hint

Don't grease your cookie sheets too heavily; it can cause cookies to spread and overbrown on the bottom.

Christmas Cookie Pops

Apple Sauce Gingerbread Cookies

4 cups all-purpose flour
2 teaspoons ground ginger
2 teaspoons ground cinnamon
1 teaspoon baking soda
½ teaspoon salt
¼ teaspoon ground nutmeg
½ cup margarine, softened
1 cup sugar
⅓ cup light (gold label) molasses
1 cup MOTT'S® Natural Apple Sauce
Decorator Icing (recipe follows)

Sift together flour, ginger, cinnamon, baking soda, salt and nutmeg; set aside. In bowl, with electric mixer at high speed, beat margarine, sugar and molasses until creamy. Alternately blend in dry ingredients and apple sauce. Cover and chill dough for several hours or overnight.

Preheat oven to 375°F. On floured surface, roll dough out to ⅛-inch thickness with lightly floured rolling pin. Cut with floured gingerbread man cutter or other shapes. Place on greased baking sheet. Bake 12 minutes or until done. Remove from sheet; cool on wire rack.

Frost with Decorator Icing as desired. After icing dries, store in airtight container.

Makes 2½ dozen (5½-inch) cookies

Decorator Icing: Mix 2 cups confectioners' sugar and 1 tablespoon water. Add more water, 1 teaspoon at a time, until icing holds its shape and can be piped through a decorating tube.

Helpful Hint

Before measuring molasses, lightly coat a measuring cup with nonstick cooking spray so the molasses will slide out easily instead of clinging to the cup.

Chocolate Reindeer

1 cup butter or margarine, softened
1 cup sugar
1 egg
1 teaspoon vanilla
2 ounces semisweet chocolate, melted
2¼ cups all-purpose flour
1 teaspoon baking powder
¼ teaspoon salt
Royal Icing (recipe follows)
Assorted small candies

1. Beat butter and sugar in large bowl at high speed of electric mixer until fluffy. Beat in egg and vanilla. Add melted chocolate; mix well. Add flour, baking powder and salt; mix well. Cover and refrigerate about 2 hours or until firm.

2. Preheat oven to 325°F. Grease 2 cookie sheets; set aside.

3. Divide dough in half. Reserve 1 half; wrap remaining dough in plastic wrap and refrigerate.

4. Roll reserved dough on well-floured surface to ¼-inch thickness. Cut with reindeer cookie cutter. Place 2 inches apart on prepared cookie sheet. Chill 10 minutes.

5. Bake 13 to 15 minutes or until set. Cool completely on cookie sheets. Repeat steps with remaining dough.

6. Prepare Royal Icing.

7. To decorate, pipe assorted colored icing on reindeer and add small candies. For best results, let cookies dry overnight uncovered before storing in airtight container at room temperature.
Makes 16 (4-inch) reindeer

Royal Icing

2 to 3 large egg whites*
2 to 4 cups powdered sugar
1 tablespoon lemon juice

*Use only grade A clean, uncracked eggs.

Beat 2 egg whites in medium bowl with electric mixer until peaks just begin to hold their shape. Add 2 cups sugar and lemon juice; beat for 1 minute. If consistency is too thin for piping, gradually add more sugar until desired result is achieved; if it is too thick, add another egg white. Divide icing among several small bowls and tint to desired colors. Keep bowls tightly covered until ready to use.

Holiday Bits Cutout Cookies

1 cup (2 sticks) butter or
  margarine, softened
1 cup sugar
2 eggs
2 teaspoons vanilla extract
2½ cups all-purpose flour
  ½ teaspoon baking powder
  ½ teaspoon salt
  HERSHEY'S® Holiday
  Candy Coated Bits

1. Beat butter, sugar, eggs and
vanilla in large bowl on low speed
of electric mixer just until blended.
Stir together flour, baking powder
and salt; add to butter mixture,
stirring until well blended.

2. Divide dough in half. Cover;
refrigerate 1 to 2 hours or until
firm enough to handle. Heat
oven to 400°F. On lightly floured
surface, roll each half of the
dough to about ¼ inch thick.

3. Cut into tree, wreath, star or
other shapes with 2½-inch cookie
cutters. Place on ungreased
cookie sheet. Press candy coated
bits into cutouts.

4. Bake 6 to 8 minutes or until
edges are firm and bottoms are
very lightly browned. Remove
from cookie sheet to wire rack.
Cool completely.

*Makes about 3½ dozen
cookies*

Prep Time: 30 minutes
Bake Time: 6 minutes
Chill Time: 1 hour

Helpful Hint

Cookies, brownies
and bars make great gifts.
Place them in a paper-lined
tin or on a decorative plate
covered with plastic wrap
and tied with colorful ribbon.
For a special touch, include
the recipe.

Holiday Bits Cutout Cookies

Extra-Special Cookies

Danish Cookie Rings

½ cup blanched almonds
2 cups all-purpose flour
¾ cup sugar
¼ teaspoon baking powder
1 cup butter, cut into small pieces
1 large egg
1 tablespoon milk
1 tablespoon vanilla
8 candied red cherries
16 candied green cherries

Grease cookie sheets; set aside. Process almonds in food processor until ground, but not pasty. Place almonds, flour, sugar and baking powder in large bowl. Cut butter into flour mixture with pastry blender or 2 knives until mixture is crumbly.

continued on page 82

Danish Cookie Rings, continued

Beat egg, milk and vanilla in small bowl with fork until well blended. Add egg mixture to flour mixture; stir until soft dough forms.

Spoon dough into pastry bag fitted with medium star tip. Pipe 3-inch rings 2 inches apart onto prepared cookie sheets. Refrigerate rings 15 minutes or until firm.

Preheat oven to 375°F. Cut cherries into halves. Cut each red cherry half into quarters; cut each green cherry half into 4 slivers. Press red cherry quarter onto each ring where ends meet. Arrange 2 green cherry slivers on either side of red cherry to form leaves. Bake 8 to 10 minutes or until golden. Remove cookies to wire racks; cool completely. Store tightly covered at room temperature or freeze up to 3 months.

Makes about 5 dozen cookies

Molded Scotch Shortbread

1½ cups all-purpose flour
¼ teaspoon salt
¾ cup butter, softened
⅓ cup sugar
1 egg

1. Preheat oven to temperature recommended by shortbread mold manufacturer. Combine flour and salt in medium bowl.

2. Beat butter and sugar in large bowl with electric mixer at medium speed until light and fluffy. Beat in egg. Gradually add flour mixture. Beat at low speed until well blended.

3. Spray 10-inch ceramic shortbread mold with nonstick cooking spray.* Press dough firmly into mold. Bake, cool and remove from mold according to manufacturer's directions.

Makes 1 shortbread mold or 24 cookies

*If mold is not available, preheat oven to 350°F. Shape tablespoonfuls of dough into 1-inch balls. Place 2 inches apart on ungreased cookie sheets; press with fork to flatten. Bake 18 to 20 minutes or until edges are lightly browned. Let cookies stand on cookie sheets 2 minutes; transfer to wire racks to cool completely. Store tightly covered at room temperature or freeze up to 3 months.

Molded Scotch Shortbread

Date Pinwheel Cookies

1¼ cups dates, pitted and
finely chopped
¾ cup orange juice
½ cup granulated sugar
1 tablespoon butter
3 cups plus 1 tablespoon all-
purpose flour, divided
2 teaspoons vanilla, divided
4 ounces cream cheese
¼ cup vegetable shortening
1 cup packed brown sugar
2 eggs
1 teaspoon baking soda
½ teaspoon salt

1. Heat dates, orange juice,
granulated sugar, butter and
1 tablespoon flour in medium
saucepan over medium heat.
Cook 10 minutes or until thick,
stirring frequently; remove from
heat. Stir in 1 teaspoon vanilla;
set aside to cool.

2. Beat cream cheese, shortening
and brown sugar in large bowl
about 3 minutes until light and
fluffy. Add eggs and remaining
1 teaspoon vanilla; beat 2
minutes longer.

3. Combine 3 cups flour, baking
soda and salt in medium bowl.
Add to shortening mixture; stir
just until blended. Divide dough
in half. Roll one half of dough on
lightly floured work surface into

12×9-inch rectangle. Spread half
of date mixture over dough.
Spread evenly, leaving ¼-inch
border on top short edge. Starting
at short side, tightly roll up dough
jelly-roll style. Wrap in plastic
wrap; freeze for at least 1 hour.
Repeat with remaining dough.

4. Preheat oven to 350°F. Grease
cookie sheets. Unwrap dough.
Using heavy thread or dental
floss, cut dough into ¼-inch
slices. Place slices 1 inch apart
on prepared cookie sheets.

5. Bake 12 minutes or until lightly
browned. Let cookies stand on
cookie sheets 2 minutes. Remove
cookies to wire rack; cool
completely.

Makes 6 dozen cookies

Date Pinwheel Cookies

Banana Crescents

½ cup DOLE® Chopped
   Almonds, toasted
6 tablespoons sugar, divided
½ cup margarine, cut into
   pieces
1½ cups plus 2 tablespoons
   all-purpose flour
⅛ teaspoon salt
1 extra-ripe, medium DOLE®
   Banana, peeled
2 to 3 ounces semisweet
   chocolate chips

• Pulverize almonds with 2 tablespoons sugar.

• Beat margarine, almonds, remaining 4 tablespoons sugar, flour and salt.

• Purée banana; add to almond mixture and mix until well blended.

• Roll tablespoonfuls of dough into logs, then shape into crescents. Place on ungreased cookie sheet. Bake in 375°F oven 25 minutes or until golden. Cool on wire rack.

• Melt chocolate in microwavable dish at MEDIUM (50% power) 1½ to 2 minutes, stirring once. Dip ends of cookies in chocolate. Refrigerate until chocolate is set.
Makes 2 dozen cookies

Mocha Biscotti

2½ cups all-purpose flour
½ cup unsweetened cocoa
2 teaspoons DAVIS® Baking
   Powder
1¼ cups sugar
¾ cup egg substitute
¼ cup margarine or butter,
   melted
4 teaspoons instant coffee
   powder
½ teaspoon vanilla extract
⅓ cup PLANTERS® Slivered
   Almonds, chopped
   Powdered sugar, optional

1. Mix flour, cocoa and baking powder in small bowl; set aside.

2. Beat sugar, egg substitute, melted margarine or butter, coffee powder and vanilla in large bowl with mixer at medium speed for 2 minutes. Stir in flour mixture and almonds.

3. Divide dough in half. Shape each portion of dough with floured hands into 14×2-inch log on a greased baking sheet. (Dough will be sticky). Bake in preheated 350°F oven for 25 minutes.

4. Remove from oven and cut each log on a diagonal into 16 (1-inch) slices. Place biscotti, cut-side up, on baking sheets; return to oven and bake 10 to 15 minutes more on each side or until lightly toasted.

5. Remove from sheets. Cool completely on wire racks. Dust biscotti tops with powdered sugar if desired. Store in airtight container. *Makes 32 biscotti*

Preparation Time: 20 minutes
Cook Time: 35 minutes
Total Time: 1 hour and 5 minutes

Chocolate-Gilded Danish Sugar Cones

½ **cup butter or margarine, softened**
½ **cup sugar**
½ **cup all-purpose flour**
2 **egg whites**
1 **teaspoon vanilla**
3 **ounces bittersweet chocolate** *or* ½ **cup semisweet chocolate chips**

Preheat oven to 400°F. Generously grease 4 cookie sheets. Beat butter and sugar in large bowl until light and fluffy. Blend in flour. In clean, dry bowl, beat egg whites until foamy. Blend into butter mixture. Add vanilla. Using teaspoon, place 4 mounds of dough 4 inches apart on each prepared cookie sheet. Spread mounds to 3-inch diameter with small spatula dipped in water.

Bake 1 sheet at a time, 5 to 6 minutes or until edges are just barely golden. (Do not overbake or cookies become crisp too quickly and are difficult to shape.) Remove from oven and quickly loosen each cookie from cookie sheet with thin spatula. Shape each cookie into a cone; cones will become firm as they cool. (If cookies become too firm to shape, return to oven for a few seconds to soften.)

Melt chocolate in small bowl over hot water. Stir until smooth. When all cookies are baked and cooled, dip wide ends into melted chocolate; let stand until chocolate is set.

Makes about 16 cookies

Linzer Sandwich Cookies

1⅓ **cups all-purpose flour**
¼ **teaspoon baking powder**
¼ **teaspoon salt**
¾ **cup granulated sugar**
½ **cup butter, softened**
1 **large egg**
1 **teaspoon vanilla**
   Powdered sugar (optional)
   Seedless raspberry jam

Place flour, baking powder and salt in small bowl; stir to combine. Beat granulated sugar and butter in medium bowl with electric mixer at medium speed until light and fluffy. Beat in egg and vanilla. Gradually add flour mixture. Beat at low speed until dough forms. Divide dough in half; cover and refrigerate 2 hours or until firm.

Preheat oven to 375°F. Working with 1 portion at a time, roll out dough on lightly floured surface to ³⁄₁₆-inch thickness. Cut dough into desired shapes with floured cookie cutters. Cut out equal numbers of each shape. (If dough becomes too soft, refrigerate several minutes before continuing.) Cut 1-inch centers out of half the cookies of each shape. Reroll trimmings and cut out more cookies. Place cookies 1½ to 2 inches apart on ungreased cookie sheets. Bake 7 to 9 minutes or until edges are lightly brown. Let cookies stand on cookie sheets 1 to 2 minutes. Remove cookies to wire racks; cool completely.

Sprinkle cookies with holes with powdered sugar, if desired. Spread 1 teaspoon jam on flat side of whole cookies, spreading almost to edges. Place cookies with holes, flat side down, over jam. Store tightly covered at room temperature or freeze up to 3 months.

Makes about 2 dozen cookies

Helpful Hint

To soften cold butter, cut a stick into ½-inch slices and place on a microwavable plate. Heat at MEDIUM-LOW (30% power) about 30 seconds.

Linzer Sandwich Cookies

Mincemeat Pastries

3½ cups all-purpose flour
¾ cup granulated sugar
½ teaspoon salt
½ cup (1 stick) butter, chilled
8 tablespoons vegetable shortening
1 cup buttermilk
1 cup mincemeat
¼ cup powdered sugar (optional)

1. Combine flour, granulated sugar and salt in large bowl; set aside.

2. Cut butter into 1-inch chunks. Add butter and shortening to flour mixture. Cut in with pastry blender or 2 knives until mixture resembles coarse crumbs. Drizzle buttermilk over top; toss just until mixture comes together into a ball.

3. Turn out dough onto lightly floured work surface; fold in half and flatten to about ½ inch thick. Knead about eight times. Divide dough in half; press each half into ½-inch-thick disk. Wrap in plastic wrap and refrigerate at least 30 minutes.

4. Preheat oven to 350°F. Lightly grease cookie sheets; set aside. Let dough rest at room temperature 10 minutes. Roll one disk of dough into 18×12-inch rectangle on lightly floured work surface. Cut into 24 (3-inch) squares. Place heaping ½ teaspoon mincemeat in center of each square. Fold one corner about ⅔ of the way over the filling; fold opposite corner ⅔ of the way over the filling.

5. Place 2 inches apart on prepared cookie sheets. Repeat with remaining dough.

6. Bake 20 minutes or until lightly browned. Remove cookies to wire rack; cool completely. Sprinkle tops of pastries lightly with powdered sugar, if desired.

Makes 4 dozen cookies

Mincemeat Pastries

Acknowledgments

The publishers would like to thank the companies and organizations listed below for the use of their recipes in this publication.

Bestfoods

Blue Diamond Growers®

Cherry Marketing Institute

Dole Food Company, Inc.

Duncan Hines® and Moist Deluxe® are registered trademarks of Aurora Foods Inc.

Fleischmann's® Original Spread

Hershey Foods Corporation

Kahlúa® Liqueur

Kellogg Company

M&M/MARS

MOTT'S® Inc., a division of Cadbury Beverages Inc.

The Procter & Gamble Company

The J.M. Smucker Company

Index

METRIC CONVERSION CHART

VOLUME MEASUREMENTS (dry)

1/8 teaspoon = 0.5 mL
1/4 teaspoon = 1 mL
1/2 teaspoon = 2 mL
3/4 teaspoon = 4 mL
1 teaspoon = 5 mL
1 tablespoon = 15 mL
2 tablespoons = 30 mL
1/4 cup = 60 mL
1/3 cup = 75 mL
1/2 cup = 125 mL
2/3 cup = 150 mL
3/4 cup = 175 mL
1 cup = 250 mL
2 cups = 1 pint = 500 mL
3 cups = 750 mL
4 cups = 1 quart = 1 L

VOLUME MEASUREMENTS (fluid)

1 fluid ounce (2 tablespoons) = 30 mL
4 fluid ounces (1/2 cup) = 125 mL
8 fluid ounces (1 cup) = 250 mL
12 fluid ounces (1 1/2 cups) = 375 mL
16 fluid ounces (2 cups) = 500 mL

WEIGHTS (mass)

1/2 ounce = 15 g
1 ounce = 30 g
3 ounces = 90 g
4 ounces = 120 g
8 ounces = 225 g
10 ounces = 285 g
12 ounces = 360 g
16 ounces = 1 pound = 450 g

DIMENSIONS

1/16 inch = 2 mm
1/8 inch = 3 mm
1/4 inch = 6 mm
1/2 inch = 1.5 cm
3/4 inch = 2 cm
1 inch = 2.5 cm

OVEN TEMPERATURES

250°F = 120°C
275°F = 140°C
300°F = 150°C
325°F = 160°C
350°F = 180°C
375°F = 190°C
400°F = 200°C
425°F = 220°C
450°F = 230°C

BAKING PAN SIZES

Utensil	Size in Inches/Quarts	Metric Volume	Size in Centimeters
Baking or Cake Pan (square or rectangular)	8×8×2	2 L	20×20×5
	9×9×2	2.5 L	23×23×5
	12×8×2	3 L	30×20×5
	13×9×2	3.5 L	33×23×5
Loaf Pan	8×4×3	1.5 L	20×10×7
	9×5×3	2 L	23×13×7
Round Layer Cake Pan	8×1½	1.2 L	20×4
	9×1½	1.5 L	23×4
Pie Plate	8×1¼	750 mL	20×3
	9×1¼	1 L	23×3
Baking Dish or Casserole	1 quart	1 L	—
	1½ quart	1.5 L	—
	2 quart	2 L	—